DUE

S

SPORTBIKES

MOTORCYCLE MANIA

David and Patricia Armentrout

Rourke

Publishing LLC
Vero Beach, Florida 32964

www.rourkepublishing.com

PHOTO CREDITS: Cover ©Getty Images; pp. 9, 15, 16, 17, 21 © Honda; title page, pp. 5, 6, 7, 13, 22 © Suzuki; pp. 11 ©BMW

Title page: *Sportbikes are stylish machines built for speed.*

Editor: Frank Sloan

Cover and page design by Nicola Stratford

Library of Congress Cataloging-in-Publication Data

Armentrout, David, 1962-
  Sportbikes / David and Patricia Armentrout.
     p. cm. -- (Motorcycle mania)
  Includes index.
  ISBN 1-59515-456-6 (hardcover)
  1. Superbikes--Juvenile literature. I. Armentrout, Patricia, 1960- II. Title. III. Series.

  TL440.15.A765 2006
  629.227'5--dc22

2005010720

Printed in the USA

CG/CG

Rourke Publishing
1-800-394-7055
www.rourkepublishing.com
sales@rourkepublishing.com
Post Office Box 3328, Vero Beach, FL 32964

TABLE OF CONTENTS

A GREAT RIDE

Motorcycle riders love riding their machines. They love nothing more than the feel of the wind on their face and the sun on their backs as they cruise down the road. They just don't get the same feeling when they ride in a car. Motorcycle riders experience their surroundings—they don't just drive through them.

A sportbike's aerodynamic shape reduces friction.

Sportbikes are street bikes that look more like racing motorcycles. And the comparison doesn't stop with looks. Sportbikes are fast, light, agile machines closely related to some types of racing bikes. Sportbikes are for riders who want high **performance** and a great looking machine.

Sportbikes are high-performance machines that should be driven with extreme care.

The twists and turns of a country road are a sportbike rider's dream.

THE PROPER GEAR

A crash on any motorcycle can be serious. Even minor accidents can leave a rider with bumps, scrapes, and bruises. Proper riding equipment can offer some protection. Minimum gear includes a long sleeve shirt or jacket and long pants made for motorcycle riders. Riders should also wear fitted boots and reinforced gloves. Most important, all riders need a full-face helmet to protect them from bugs, rain, and of course a bump on the head.

For extra protection, motorcycle racers add **body armor** made of hard plastic and foam rubber.

A pro racer wears protective clothing with padded armor.

MOUNT UP

At first glance, sportbike riders don't look very comfortable. The riders are positioned so they lean forward with their feet trailing behind them. The awkward riding position actually allows riders to ride low and close to the bike, giving them better control.

Leaning low and close to a bike minimizes wind resistance.

A FAST ROAD MACHINE

Sportbikes may not be the best choice for new riders. The bikes are very fast and **responsive**. New riders may be caught off guard by the explosive power sportbikes are capable of. A sportbike can reach speeds of more than 100 miles (161 kilometers) an hour in just seconds. However, sportbikes can be just as safe as any other motorcycle provided riders ride responsibly.

Inexperienced riders who show off on their bikes or ride irresponsibly are called squids.

Sportbike owners can benefit from taking riding courses before hitting the streets.

SPORTBIKE RACING

Fans and riders alike love sportbike racing. Sportbike racers ride motorcycles that are nearly identical to **production** motorcycles. This gives fans something in common with the racers. Since only slight changes to the bikes are allowed, sportbike racers must rely on skill to win a race.

A sportbike is light and responsive, allowing a racer to easily lean into curves.

Superbike racing motorcycles are similar to sportbikes, but are **modified** with expensive high-performance parts for racing. Superbikes are much faster than production bikes. Racers can reach speeds close to 200 miles (322 kilometers) an hour. Riders circle the track attacking corners and leaning into curves so low their knees scrape the pavement.

Superbike racers wear plastic or leather pads called knee sliders to protect their knees when cornering.

AMA (American Motorcycle Association) road racing was first organized in 1934.

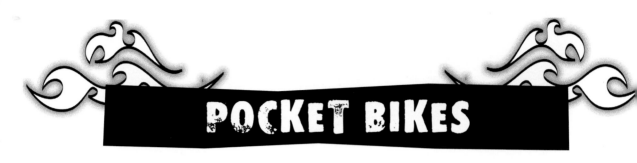

POCKET BIKES

Pocket bikes are the newest things in motorcycling. Pocket bikes look like miniature sportbikes. Riders sit just a foot or two off the ground in a crunched up position. However, pocket bikes are not toys. Many can go 50 miles (80.5 kilometers) per hour or more. It is not legal or safe to ride pocket bikes on the road. The best place to ride a pocket bike is on an approved track.

Pocket bike racing is popular in many parts of the world.

Kids love to ride pocket bikes, but they should always have adult supervision.

BEST SELLERS

In recent years, sportbikes have become one of the best selling types of motorcycles. Manufacturers like Honda, Ducati, Yamaha, and Kawasaki make many different models to satisfy riders all over the world.

Sportbikes are powerful machines and should be ridden by experienced riders. Fortunately, many dealers offer riding and safety courses for new riders.

If a laid-back riding style is not your thing, then a sportbike may be right for you.

The World's Fastest Production Motorcycle

Suzuki GSX1300R Hayabusa

Named after the Japanese word for Peregrine Falcon

Top Speed = 194 miles (312 kilometers) per hour
0-60 miles (97 kilometers) per hour = 2.6 seconds
Engine = 1299 cubic centimeter, 4 stroke, 4 cycle
Length = 84.3 inches (2140 millimeters)
Width = 29.1 inches (740 millimeters)
Height = 45.5 inches (1155 millimeters)
Weight = 478 pounds (217 kilograms)

GLOSSARY

body armor (BOD ee AR mur) — protective clothing worn by motorcycle racers

modified (MOD uh fyde) — changed from its original condition

performance (pur FOR muhns) — the way something works

production (pruh DUK shun) — bikes built for sale to the general public

responsive (re SPON siv) — quick to react

INDEX

FURTHER READING

Graham, Ian. *Super Bikes: Designed for Success*. Heinemann Library, 2003.
Hill, Lee Sullivan. *Motorcycles*. Lerner Publications, 2004.
Jefferis, David. *Super Bikes: Monster Machines*. Raintree, 2003.

WEBSITES TO VISIT

American Motorcyclist Association
   www.ama-cycle.org/
British Superbike Organization
   www.britishsuperbike.com/

ABOUT THE AUTHORS

David and Patricia Armentrout specialize in writing nonfiction books for young readers. They have had several books published for primary school reading. The Armentrouts live in Cincinnati, Ohio, with their two children.